Experiments Explained

By Cecilia Ochoa
Illustrated by Romulo Reyes III

Library For All Ltd.

Library For All is an Australian not for profit organisation with a mission to make knowledge accessible to all via an innovative digital library solution. Visit us at libraryforall.org

Experiments Explained

This edition published 2022

Published by Library For All Ltd
Email: info@libraryforall.org
URL: libraryforall.org

This work is licensed under the Creative Commons Attribution-NonCommercial-NoDerivatives 4.0 International License. To view a copy of this license, visit http://creativecommons.org/licenses/by-nc-nd/4.0/.

Library For All gratefully acknowledges the contributions of all who made previous editions of this book possible.

This book was made possible by the generous support of Save The Children.

Original illustrations by Romulo Reyes III

Experiments Explained
Ochoa, Cecilia
ISBN: 978-1-922835-12-3
SKU02703

Experiments Explained

What is an Experiment?

Have you ever wondered about something, made a guess, and then took action to see if your guess was right? If you have, then you have done a simple experiment.

Experiments help people to find answers to questions that interest them. The questions experiments try to answer can be simple. For example, a child might wonder what an onion tastes like, and then bite into it to find out.

Often, though, experiments try to answer more complicated problems. Experiments can test ideas so important that the result can help to change our world. Famous scientists like Galileo, Newton, Marie Curie, and Einstein used experiments that allow us understand the way the world works.

Scientific Method

An experiment is an important part of the scientific method, the process researchers use to answer questions or test new ideas. There are typically seven steps in the scientific method:

1. State the problem or question.

2. Find out more about the question's topic through initial observations or background research.

3. Come up with an informed guess or hypothesis based on what you found out in step 2.

4. Do an experiment to test the hypothesis.

5. Collect and analyze the results from the experiment.

6. Come to a conclusion based on the results.

7. Communicate the findings.

Elements of an Experiment

In an experiment, a researcher looks at different factors to come to a precise and accurate conclusion. These factors are also called variables.

Types of Variables

Independent variable: Something that is changed or adjusted within an experiment

Dependent variable: Something that the experiment's hypothesis expects will be affected by changes in the independent variable

Constant variable: Something that is kept unchanged throughout the experiment to make sure that it is only the effect of the independent variable that is being observed

watering seeds   not watering seeds

A change in one of the variables can cause the results to change. Thus, experiments need to be careful about how they work with these variables.

In scientific experiments, researchers will set up and observe a situation where the independent variable is not changed. This is called a control. By doing this, researchers can see if it is really the independent variable that is creating the result.

Experimental Observation *Control Observation*

Researchers also make several observations or trials within an experiment. By making more than one observation of the same set of conditions, an experiment reduces the possibility that the result was an accident or a fluke.

Why Experiments Matter

Every invention that we depend on today—from the medicine we take to the gadgets we use—is the result of a series of experiments. We advance as a people through this constant process of asking, testing, and learning.

Experiments are the basis of human knowledge. We know things to be true because repeated trials have proven them to be true. Experiments also move our learning forward by figuring out answers to things we do not know, or things we do not know for sure.

Is there a question you are puzzling over? Do you think you have a solution to a problem, but you're not sure if it will really work? Did you read about another experiment, and want to see for yourself if their conclusion was right? Ask a teacher or parent to help you. Experiment and learn!

Experiments That Kids Can Do

- **Potatoes in Salt Water vs. Fresh Water:** Cut a potato in two. (Ask an adult to help you.) Prepare two deep containers of water: one with salt (about a tablespoon or so), and another without salt. Put one potato piece (cut side down) into each of the two containers and observe the difference between the two pieces after a few hours. Why do you think there is a difference? *(Hint: This experiment is about osmosis.)*

- **Limes or Lemons in Water:** Put a lime or lemon with the rind on in a bowl of water. What happens? Now peel the rind off of the fruit and put it in water. What happens now? What ideas come to mind after this experiment? *(Hint: You may want to read the booklet on things that float.)*

- **Volcano of Vinegar:** It would be best to do this experiment outdoors. Place a tablespoon of baking soda (sodium bicarbonate) in a container. Pour some vinegar over the baking soda and stand back. What happens? Why do you think that happened? *(Hint: This experiment is about the reaction between an acid and a base.)*

Glossary

Complicated: difficult; involves many different parts; hard to understand

Conclusion: an answer reached after thinking about one's findings

Dependent: needing or relying on something else

Fluke: something that happened once and only by chance or accident

Hypothesis: an initial answer or explanation that needs to be proven true or false

Observation: information based on what you see, hear, notice, or record

Research: systematic way to study or learn about something

Trials: attempts to observe something in an experiment

Copyright-free images used in this publication were sourced from Public Domain sources and the following Creative Commons-licensed materials:

By Martin Cron (kid scientist) [CC BY-NC 2.0 (https://creativecommons.org/licenses/by-nc/2.0/)] via Flickr

References:

- Science fair project - what is an experiment? (sciencekidsathome.com)
- Kids science: Learn about the Scientific Method (ducksters.com)
- Experiment – Wikipedia
- http://www.sefmd.org/Seminar/2013/Scientific_Method%20L.%20Taylor.ppt
- Scientific_Method L. Taylor.ppt (live.com)
- Source for 'Experiments that kids can do': http://www.schoolofdragons.com/resources/)

You can use these questions to talk about this book with your family, friends and teachers.

What did you learn from this book?

Describe this book in one word. Funny? Scary? Colourful? Interesting?

How did this book make you feel when you finished reading it?

What was your favourite part of this book?

download our reader app
getlibraryforall.org

About the contributors

Library For All works with authors and illustrators from around the world to develop diverse, relevant, high quality stories for young readers. Visit libraryforall.org for the latest news on writers' workshop events, submission guidelines and other creative opportunities.

Did you enjoy this book?

We have hundreds more expertly curated original stories to choose from.

We work in partnership with authors, educators, cultural advisors, governments and NGOs to bring the joy of reading to children everywhere.

Did you know?

We create global impact in these fields by embracing the United Nations Sustainable Development Goals.

libraryforall.org

www.ingramcontent.com/pod-product-compliance
Lightning Source LLC
Chambersburg PA
CBHW040315050426
42452CB00018B/2849